I AM
TRYING

Sofia Romulan

Thank you for choosing to read my book

I hope you like it

If you do like it, would you be kind enough to rate it and leave a review. That would mean the world to me.

Thank you

Behind the door

Behind the door
Lies a big scary monster
Sometimes it knocks
Sometimes it roars
Sometimes it punches through
the walls

Sometimes I try to fight
Gather my strength and bite
With all my might
Try to scare away
The fear inside me

Other times I succumb
I let it eat all the light
Let it drag me to the darkness
of my mind
Imprison me in a cell
All alone
With only my own demons
To accompany me

All the light feels so far away

Under the stars

The happiest I feel
is when I am alone
Finally I can be real
Like a king on a throne
I have nothing to fear

No more hiding
Behind fake smiles
No more abiding
By the rules they require
I will dance around the fire
Show my true desire
Like a king on a throne

I will sing so loud
The birds will be proud
I will cry and cry
I will gaze at the sky
With an enlightened eye

The road is filled with fog
I am scared that my decision
will be wrong

Can't see the right way
Maybe I should just stay
Maybe I could just rest for today

A minute feels like an hour
I feel so drained
Locked in a tower
Contained, constrained
With no power

Why is it taking so much time?
Why is it taking so long?
A never ending climb
I am not strong
I am way past my prime

Searching for an exit
A way through the turmoil
Of my mind
A ship to help me traverse
The storm raging in my heart
An end to the demons
Clinging, Haunting, Adhering
To my soul
Affecting everything I see
Everything is in black and white
Looking for a light house
To show me a little light
Just a little bit of hope
To help me pass through the nights

At the end of the tunnel

A door will appear

One word is enough

One wrong word

At the wrong time

Is enough

To tip the scale

At the end I will be alone
At the end nothing is certain
Nothing is known
My life is hidden
Behind a curtain
Can't distinguish the false
From the truth
Did all that happen in my youth ?
Am I dreaming?
Trying to give meaning
To a life spent in vain
Full of invisible pain

Inside an empty castle
Surrounded by big walls
I live

Behind the mirror
I see their laughs
I try to mimic their smiles
Show them love
That I don't deserve
Prioritize their pain
Over my own
To feed on their praise
To feel needed
To feel important

Silence is my home
Where I can safely roam
Inside my concrete dome

black/white

In a constant state of turmoil
Not knowing whether to stop
Or continue
Whether to live or die
Whether to do or to halt
Feeling completely drained
While doing nothing
Fighting against the tide
While everyone is swimming with it
Time feels stationary
While fleeting for everyone
Accomplishments are passing by me
While I am still the same

I am cracking
Piece by piece
I am breaking
Falling apart
Can't continue the act
Wish I can finally hear the word
Cut
Or see
The end

I am rotting from the inside
The smell is no more a thing
That I can hide

I try to pass the time
After each fall
Again and again I try to climb

But I am fighting against the tide
Alone
With no guide

I cast away my pride
To ask for help
I know I won't find

Aimless I wander
Through the empty streets
I ponder

What is my goal ?
Do I have a role ?

Searching for the way
For an answer
I pray

I am scared to pass
Too scared to shine and surpass
Content on being a sheep
among the herd and sleep

Forget all the doubts
Close my eyes
So I won't see all the routes

Buried deep inside
You will find
A treasure so rare
You can't hide

Under layers of illusion
Behind years of confusion
Hidden behind the scars
It will shine like the stars

When I was away
From you
I couldn't find the way
Couldn't pass through

Couldn't see the moon
To the smell of flowers
I was immune
Feel the sun on my skin
Hide the pain within
- Until I met you

In gatherings I will be there
Hiding behind a sheath
Showing that I care
Hiding the truth beneath

I try to hold
On a thin string
That tells me I belong

At the end
All that is left is me
To keep me company

Underneath the stars
I will stay
Underneath the sun
I will raise my hand
And pray
That you will be mine

I eat and I eat
My life is on repeat
I am Dancing
to their beat

The colors disappear
when you leave
Everything I hold dear
Becomes unclear

I am waiting
For you
To notice
Me blooming
Like a lotus

Everywhere I look
I see you there
Every breath I took
I felt you in the air
In my blood stream
You give me strength
You appear in me every dream
    -My Muse

Everything I dreamt of
I found in you
You changed my view

At the end

All that remains is me

Their remains

Scattered around

Revolving around

Reminding me of the void

They used to occupy

After the rain

Comes a rainbow

From black and white

To every available color

Everyone around me is moving so fast
I have to run or I will end up being last
Scared that my prime has passed

I'll raise my voice and speak
An experience so unique
I'll seek
Against the injustice
I'll speak, I'll critique

In my own mind
I wonder
Will I ever improve
Do I have something to prove

I swim in my thoughts
Trying to find an answer
Beneath all the rubble
The sunken ships
Behind all the struggle
I inquire
For a solution I know I require
To be able to continue the fight
I need to lit my own fire

I go to therapy and speak
Baring all my truth
With no reserve
But as soon as I get out
I feel the layers of shame
Covering me from head to toe
Someone other than you knows
Knows the truth
Knows your true thoughts
My inner demons emerge
From hiding
Baring their fangs
Erasing all my reasoning
All the progress disappears
Leaving me alone
With my scary thoughts

The fear of loneliness
Is nothing
Compared to the fear
Of responsibility
Of commitment
Of being with some one
For eternity
The fear of disappointing them
Not living up to their expectations
Staying in your lane
That is why
Forever lonely I'll be

I can hear them
Behind my back
Their fake smiles
Flickers in my mind
Giving me many sleepless nights
Trying to deceive me
Why do I care
To this degree

I try to learn
Build a wall around
To hide
My true self
I try again and again
Try to fake smile
Offer false love
Try to beguile
But, at the end I can't
I lose every time
The wall gets broken
My true self has already spoken
    - *I can't pretend to be someone else*

Watching a seed grow
Sprouting alone
So slow
Day after day
I water and I watch
I can't take my eyes away
Something so serene
Like nothing my eyes has ever seen
Bit by bit it grows
From black to brown to green
A beautiful scene
Like the birth of a queen
But no one knows
Its hidden away
In a place only I can stay
I want to share
Make the world aware
Of the beauty in my care
she is quiet and shy
It is so easy to make her cry
So I keep her locked away
-Safe

The anger inside me
Grows with no limit
I try to keep it at bay
Imprison it behind closed doors
Behind impregnable walls
I am starting to fail
Cracks I hear
Cracks I see
Now is not the time
For it to be free

Born with no choice

Concerns I couldn't voice

A role I found my self in

A suit not in my size

Externally, it fits

Internally it hurts

Filled with thorns

My heart mourns

For the lie

I have to live

So that I can survive

Do you get it
No one will understand
Get it
You will be banned
More than you already are
You wont be able to get far
In the dark
You will be a star
At you they will bark
Try to silence you
Their thoughts will be daggers
 trying to hurt you
Will you have the courage to shine
Or let them pass through
Dim your light
And hide behind

A shackled freedom
As I walk envied by others
I am a prisoner
A shackle around my heart
A shackle around my mind
I am a coward
As I can't face the truth
I can't raise my voice
I do have a choice
But I can't face the consequences
The anxiety
This society
So I stay
Pretending to be happy
In my own shackles

Scenes from my past

Haunt me

When I am awake

And in my sleep

The little time that I dare

To sleep

They come when least expected

To eat at my sanity

Drowning me

In my thoughts

Are you waiting

For me to go home

For a minute, please stop debating

Tell me you will be waiting

When I ring the bell

Will you open the door

Please do tell

Why have you forsaken me

And my prayers you ignore

I know you love all

But I don't feel that anymore

I run

Through mud and water

I traverse

Against the wind

I swim

To the bottom of the sea

To hide

In a place I can't be found

These demons that live in me
These ghosts that haunt me
Are mine
My creations, my manifestations
My jailers, my neighbors

Searching for a home
Where I can be free
Chasing a dream
To find a key
- To my final home

I fear the storms
Long before they come
I prepare and prepare
I open my door
I offer a chair
I let them in
Too deep
Until they grow
Beyond my control
They dig in deeper
Searching for more
Their friends that I hid
Inside

With every breath I take
I remember every mistake
I made
I hide and pretend to sleep
But I cant hide the truth
That I am always awake

All the years I have been alive
In one place I've lived
A place I learned to call home
But now I don't know

I wonder and ponder
Sometimes when I open my eyes
I feel like a stranger
An unwanted guest
In my own home

Other times its okay
I don't want to hide away
I feel it fits
I decorate and paint
Many invitations I distribute
Wanting to show off
Wanting to let people how proud I am
Of my home

And then it hits me again
This tiny prickling pain
At the back of my mind
Reminding me to hide
Close the curtains and the blinds
- And stay safe inside

For every situation
There is a different me
A united front is what they see
All existing
conflicting
A perfect harmony
A dangerous balance
I am maintaining

A me who pretends
A me who blends
Hides the pain
The anger
A smile he maintains

And a me who hides away
Behind closed doors
And prays
Scared to be found
Scared to be known

Since it was a small seed
I've watched it grown
From mere doubts
It has become something
I can call my own

A mere thought
has sprung wings
With a proud voice
It sings

Loud and clear
Just enough
To make the whole world
Hear

I am falling down
In my deep thoughts
I drown

I search for a savior
A hand to help me up
To get me out
Of this swamp

I am my own helper
I only can swim
In this hell of darkness
I only can walk
On the thorns of my demons
I only can climb
Against the walls of hatred
- To be free

In my sleepless nights
I search for the naked truth
It its true form
Pure without any stains

Why am I here
In this place
In this body
Is this my true me
Do I belong I here
Right now in this space
That I don't feel is my own
A space rejecting me so hard
I have to cut it apart
So I can breathe

To all the ghosts inside
You were born of me
Fed on my desires and fears
I wish to bid you farewell
But I can't bear to say goodbye

The door is so wide open
But I am scared to pass through
Hindered by my inner shackles
That cloud my view

I am sitting here frozen
From fear, that's the risk
For the path I've chosen
I wish I could drink
So for a minute I could forget
The emotions fighting inside me

They praise me
You stand so tall
I can hide the real truth
Beguiling them all

All the signs were there
Every one could see the lightning
While all were waiting for the thunder
It never came

It got scared
By all the anticipating eyes
It became shy
Knowing it was all alone
Knowing it will be loud
Knowing it will cut the deep silence
It hesitated
To come
To make itself heard

I am all alone
In the dark
Stumbling
Please find me
Tell me it will be okay
It gets better
Comfort me
Reach out your hand
Let me hold it
Be my guide out of the dark
Embrace me
I promise
I won't rely on you
All the way
I just need a little bit of help
To find myself

All the things I tried to hide
The things I fought to forget
The things I was forced to neglect
Were there
Safe and sound
Behind the closed door
I chose to ignore

I can see them
But dare I move through
I can feel the happiness inside
Calling out my name
But the road to the door
Is filled with thorns
Condescending glares
Penetrating my sight
Whenever I try to look for my door

I am charged
Of abuse
Abusing myself
The way I tell myself
How small I am
How weak I am
I deserve no love
I deserve to be alone
I have to stop
Berating
Neglecting
My true self
I have to start accepting
Before expecting others to do the same

They offer me flowers

They hide the thorns so well

They have worked for hours

To hide them I can tell

They offer smiles that kill

They have so much skill

How many others have they fooled

I chose to forget
The abuse
I have met

Hide it deep
Behind locks and keys
So that I can fall asleep

Their knocks I ignore
Every night I hear
Trying to break the door

Am I just trading
A cage for another
Is this me getting fooled
To open the wrong door

Living another masked truth
Having a momentary peace
That I will regret

I lack the faith
To leap
My own weakness
I reap

Jumping is what I want
What I need
But I fear
The result is not guaranteed

I should stop caring
What others think
I should be daring
And let their thoughts sink

I should be strong
I might be wrong
But I won't know
Unless I try

I am trying

Sometimes I needed to see
The kindness you showed
You gave other
Whether it was fake or real
I wanted it to be mine
To be directed
Towards my soul
So that I might get fooled
In thinking that you loved me

You expect warmth
So you hold your hand
Out

You search for comfort
In a world where
It is easier to hate
To be mean

Instead you should search
Inside you
Insider the darkness
Of your heart
For that little spark
That kept you moving on

Projecting the good in you
Onto others
Expecting other to behave
The way you do
To try to be kind
To believe in the goodness
of the world
But not everyone cares
Not everyone is free
And you become disappointed
Depressed
- My mind playing tricks on me

I search for a place
Where I can be me
A place that accepts
My overwhelming love
A place where my loud
Laugh will be celebrated
Not shunned
Where my quirks will be accepted
Where my kindness
Will be reciprocated
Will be mirrored
A place where it is safe
To be me
To be my true me

Things stay the same
Some people are good
Some are bad
Please just shut up
How am I suppose to differentiate
They are the same
Why do I open myself
To the bad people only
Can't I see the signs
Am I so blindly in love
Can't I hear the demons trailing
Behind them
Can't I smell the rotten corpses
In their trail
Am I trying hard enough ?

A butterfly I was expected to be
A pretty thing that has to be fed
To bloom

A butterfly expected to soar
Spread its wings
Across the sky

They would point at me and say
Look at what we made
A creature so heavenly
No one has ever seen

Instead I chose to be a larvae
Walk on the dirty ground
Eat leaves that no body wanted
But I am starting to feel happy
Finding my own way